This is the true story of Natumi, a little orphan elephant.
She was shy and often afraid. No one ever thought Natumi
would grow up to be a leader.

Natumi
Takes the Lead

The True Story of an Orphan
Elephant Who Finds Family

Gerry Ellis with Amy Novesky

NATIONAL GEOGRAPHIC
WASHINGTON, D.C.

One spring morning on the African savanna, a little elephant, only a few weeks old, followed her herd to a watering hole for a drink. Like most elephant families, hers was very close. She never wandered more than a trunk's length away. The days were growing warmer, and the little elephant nestled in the shade beneath her mother.

Suddenly shots rang out, and a high-pitched trumpet shook the air. Elephants stampeded and scattered. Some fell. All except one.

Alone and without a mother, the little elephant ran until she was rescued by a kind farmer and taken to an elephant orphanage.

The little elephant was hungry but otherwise unharmed. As the weeks passed, other orphans arrived with wounds: sunburned skin and scratches, snake bites and bruises. And all of the elephants seemed to have broken hearts, which were the most difficult wounds to heal.

The keepers at the orphanage named the little elephant Natumi. She was a shy girl and often hid behind her keepers' legs.

And she was not alone. There were seven other orphans, each given a name—Edie, Icholta, Ilingwesi, Laikipia, Lolokwe, Nyiro, and Salama.

Soon these eight little elies would form a new family.

The names in this book can be hard to pronounce. Use this guide to help.

Natumi—NAH-too-mee
Edie—AY-dee
Icholta—EE-shohl-tah
Ilingwesi—EE-LIN-gway-zee
Laikipia—LI-kih-pee-ah
Lolokwe—loh-LOH-kway
Nyiro—en-YEAR-oh
Salama—SAH-lah-mah

Before long, life at the orphanage settled into a comforting routine. Every morning the elephants and their keepers woke in the stables. The little elies drank bottles of milk and ate copra cake, a tasty treat made from coconut meal.

Mornings in the highlands were deliciously cool. Doves cooed, distant lions roared, and curious elephants headed into the bush to explore and play.

When the East African sun was high and hot, Natumi and the other elephants bathed in mud puddles, slipping and splashing in the squishy ochre earth. Then, nice and cool, they napped in the shade of blooming acacia trees, the only sounds in the air the hum of insects and the gentle slaps of wet elephant ears.

At the end of the day, when the sky glowed purple and the heat receded, the elephants chased each other back to the stables for the night. Evenings were alive with the chatter of birds and the scent of ipomoea blossoms, wood smoke, and red dirt.

Sometimes, the rambunctious elephants didn't want to go to bed. But their keepers helped settle them down, covering them with handmade blankets.

Lala salama—good night, Edie, Icholta, Ilingwesi, Laikipia, Lolokwe, Nyiro, Salama. *Lala salama*, Natumi.

The days passed and the little elephants grew bigger and stronger. Now not-so-little Natumi tossed her keeper into the air when she tried to hide behind his legs. And she was tall enough to grab his hat.

Natumi and the other orphans had become a family, and their family needed a leader, just like in the wild. Someone to protect them and keep them safe. Who would it be?

Some keepers thought it would be brave Edie. Others guessed it would be playful Ilingwesi. No one really thought about Natumi. The keepers saw her as the shy one.

One morning, Natumi and her family headed out into the hills, trunk to tail, trunk to tail. Despite their closeness, it was easy to get lost in the thick brush.

Suddenly a high-pitched trumpet shook the air! Elephants stampeded and scattered. Some fell. But soon, all of the little elephants raced back to the clearing where their blankets and milk bottles hung. All except one.

The keepers counted the elephants—Edie, Icholta, Ilingwesi, Laikipia, Lolokwe, Nyiro, Salama. Seven elephants.

Where was Natumi?

All of a sudden, Natumi crashed through the bushes, her ears flared wide and defiant, her trunk arched above her head. She trumpeted noisily!

"Shh, Natumi, *wey wey*—it's okay," a keeper tried to reassure her. The other orphans gently touched Natumi, entwining their trunks together, rumbling gently, comforting her.

But something had changed. Natumi seemed bigger, bolder, and in fact, she was now taller than the rest.

That evening, Natumi led her family from the clearing back home.

And the next day and the next, Natumi led her family into the hills to play. She led them to the mud puddles to bathe. And she led them back home again.

One day, while the elephants were napping, Natumi trumpeted loudly, saving the elies from a snake she'd spotted above them.

Soon everyone knew: Natumi had taken the lead.

Years passed and the elies were not so little anymore. They no longer drank milk from bottles, and they were growing new teeth and tusks. The time had come for Natumi's family to leave the orphanage together for a new, wilder place. A protected park they could call home.

In the cool twilight, Natumi let the other seven elies board the truck first. As she waited, her keeper gently blew into her trunk to calm her. When all were settled and safe, Natumi climbed aboard.

And when the eight not-so-little elephants arrived at their new home, Natumi proudly led her family off of the truck and back into the wild.

Natumi's home
and where elephants live in Africa

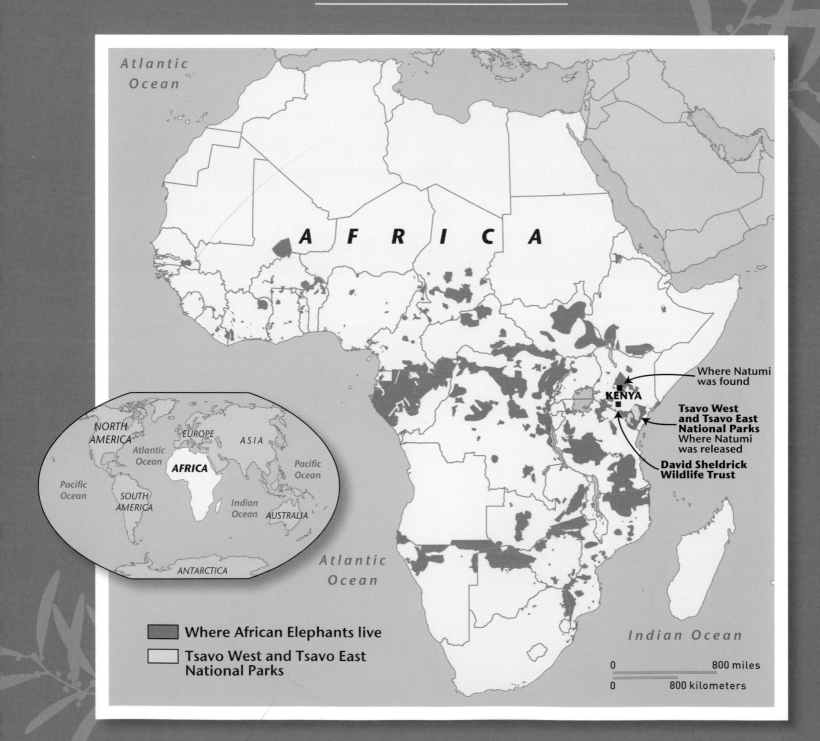

Atlantic Ocean

A F R I C A

Where Natumi
was found

KENYA

**Tsavo West
and Tsavo East
National Parks**
Where Natumi
was released

**David Sheldrick
Wildlife Trust**

*Atlantic
Ocean*

Indian Ocean

NORTH
AMERICA

*Atlantic
Ocean*

EUROPE

ASIA

AFRICA

*Pacific
Ocean*

*Pacific
Ocean*

SOUTH
AMERICA

*Indian
Ocean*

AUSTRALIA

ANTARCTICA

■ **Where African Elephants live**

☐ **Tsavo West and Tsavo East
National Parks**

0   800 miles

0   800 kilometers

Want to learn more about elephants?

ABOUT THE DAVID SHELDRICK WILDLIFE TRUST

The David Sheldrick Wildlife Trust is the world's most successful elephant rescue and rehabilitation center. Since Dr. Dame Daphne Sheldrick first founded it in 1977, she and the keepers at the Trust have hand-raised more than 190 young elephants who lost their families. After they've grown, these once orphaned elephants return to live with the wild elephant herds in Tsavo East National Park. Want to learn more? With the help of a parent, you can go online and learn about the Trust's many other conservation programs and even foster one of the elephants to help with their rescue missions. Visit sheldrickwildlifetrust.org for more information.

WEBSITES

National Geographic Kids and Education
Fact pages, photos, and range maps for kids, parents, and educators

education.nationalgeographic.com/topics/elephants

kids.nationalgeographic.com/animals/african-elephant

***National Geographic* Magazine**
Read an article and check out a photo gallery of orphans living at the David Sheldrick Wildlife Trust.

ngm.nationalgeographic.com/2011/09/orphan-elephants/siebert-text

World Elephant Day
A campaign that celebrates elephants every August 12, bringing attention to the challenges elephants face today

worldelephantday.org

BOOKS

Blewett, Ashlee Brown. *Mission Elephant Rescue*. National Geographic Kids Books, 2014.

Ellis, Gerry. *Wild Orphans*. Welcome Books, 2002.

Joubert, Dereck, and Beverly Joubert. *Face to Face With Elephants*. National Geographic Kids Books, 2008.

Marsh, Laura. *National Geographic Kids Readers: Great Migrations, Elephants*. National Geographic Kids Books, 2010.

O'Connell, Caitlin, and Donna M. Jackson. *The Elephant Scientist*. HMH Books for Young Readers, 2011.

Sheldrick, Daphne. *Love, Life, and Elephants*. Picador, 2013.

Facts About Elephants

- Because ivory is so valuable to some humans, many elephants have been killed for their tusks. This trade is illegal today, but it has not been completely eliminated, and some African elephant populations remain endangered.
- Elephants eat roots, grasses, fruit, and bark. An adult elephant can consume up to 300 pounds (136 kg) of food in a single day.
- Mother elephants use their trunks to lift newborns to their feet.
- Elephants can hear each other trumpet up to five miles (8 km) away.
- African elephants have ears shaped like the continent of Africa.
- Elephants sometimes make purr-like sounds when content.

ELEPHANT GROWTH

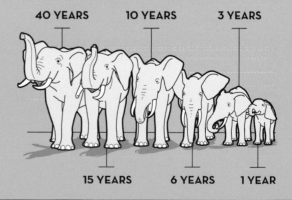

40 YEARS   10 YEARS   3 YEARS

15 YEARS   6 YEARS   1 YEAR

The world's largest land mammal, elephants in the wild can live up to 70 years. Natumi was only 6 weeks old when she was rescued, and today Natumi would only be a teenager, about 16 years old.

A note from the photographer

A keeper feeds Natumi and her family a breakfast of copra cake, made from dried coconut, before heading out into the African bush to explore for the day.

My passion for African elephants stretches back more than 25 years, to my first trip to East Africa. When I saw my first elephant herd grazing on the savanna, they seemed as big as the landscape—everything I imagined they would be.

Of the thousands of elephants I have seen and photographed across the African continent, ironically it was one of the smallest, Natumi, who stood apart because of what she taught me about her species. And because of her, my passion and love for elephants grew immensely. Not just as wild symbols of Africa, but as kindred spirits in a shared world. Even though humans and elephants look so different, remarkably, we share so much: compassion, joy, sadness, curiosity, fear, parental instincts, even humor.

Getting the chance to photograph Natumi and the other orphans at the David Sheldrick Wildlife Trust was an experience I'll never forget. From little daily experiences, such as waking up to Natumi's wet trunk tip running across my face (the elephant way of identifying me) to seeing keepers do amazing things, such as bravely rescuing young elephants from the brink of death, or calming the little ones when they were afraid or lonely.

Natumi was one of the lucky orphans; she survived her ordeal and was rescued. In 1999, the year I began photographing at the David Sheldrick Wildlife Trust, nearly a dozen orphans appeared instead of the usual two or three. A combination of renewed poaching, prolonged drought, and human-elephant conflict caused a boom of babies without mothers. Today, elephants still face dire threats such as these, and we must do everything in our power to make sure no other elephant babies go motherless.

Every so often, some elephants, Natumi included, return to visit their human family. Though the keepers haven't spotted her in a few years since she left the orphanage, we hope Natumi has been living in harmony with her new elephant family. However, many endangered elephants still need the love, family, and security that Natumi has found—and there is much that we can do to help them. While humans have been the source of conflict for many elephants, we can also join efforts to be their protectors and their friends—and even sometimes their families.

In photographing Natumi and the other seven little orphans, my connection with elephants expanded in many ways that I never anticipated when I began. A huge debt of gratitude goes to all the keepers, including Mishak, Edwin, and Patrick, for the extraordinary amount of unseen work that they do each day and also for what they shared with me during my time in Nairobi and Tsavo National Parks.

I also cannot begin to thank Daphne Sheldrick and her daughters, Jill and Angela, for the kindness that they shared with me and for the openness with which they allowed me to photograph for several years in order to create this rare collection of images that tell Natumi's story and bring to light the lives of the little "orphan eight." Without their generosity, none of these photos, or my intimate connection with elephants, would exist.

—Gerry Ellis

Photographer Gerry Ellis shares a moment with ten-month-old Nyiro, a member of Natumi's new family, at the David Sheldrick Wildlife Trust.

Credits

For Jenn—whose curiosity, passion, and caring for Earth's creatures, large and small, has helped me see the world through more understanding and loving eyes. —G.E.

For the elephants and all of those brave and generous souls who work to save them. May this book inspire even more. —A.N.

NATIONAL GEOGRAPHIC and Yellow Border Design are trademarks of the National Geographic Society, used under license.

For more information, visit www.natgeo.com/info, call 1-800-647-5463, or write to the following address:

National Geographic Partners
1145 17th Street N.W.
Washington, D.C. 20036-4688 U.S.A.

Visit us online at nationalgeographic.com/books

For librarians and teachers: ngchildrensbooks.org

More for kids from National Geographic:
kids.nationalgeographic.com

For information about special discounts for bulk purchases, please contact National Geographic Books Special Sales: ngspecsales@ngs.org

For rights or permissions inquiries, please contact National Geographic Books Subsidiary Rights: ngbookrights@ngs.org

Designed by Callie Broaddus

Trade hardcover ISBN: 978-1-4263-2561-8
Reinforced library binding ISBN: 978-1-4263-2562-5

Printed in Hong Kong
16/THK/1

Unless otherwise noted, all photos © Gerry Ellis/Minden Pictures. Page 32: (LE), Tierney Farrell; (RT), Graeme Shannon/Shutterstock.

A NOTE ON THE DESIGN

Natumi was found and rescued near Nanyuki, a town in Kenya, Africa, situated at the base of the country's tallest peak, Mount Kenya. Much of the imagery found in these pages is inspired by the landscape of that area, including the illustrations of acacia trees and elephant grass, both of which wild elephants love to eat.

The bright colors and geometric patterns in the book are influenced by the jewelry and dress of local cultures, including the Samburu, many of whom live just north of where Natumi was found. The Samburu are also known as the Butterfly People, because of the bright and beautiful colors they often wear.

Left: Samburu tribe woman
Right: Acacia tree on African savanna